10 Unaccompanied Duets for E♭ Instruments (Alto Saxophone and others)

Gospel For Two

Table of Contents

● Demo version

 Play-along version (second part only)

CURNOW®
MUSIC

Order Number: CMP 1225-07-400

James Curnow
GOSPEL FOR TWO
E♭ Instruments

ISBN: 978-90-431-2863-6

CD number: 19-092-3 CMP

Gospel For Two

Ten Unaccompanied Duets in a Gospel style
For any instruments

Greetings!

Music has no boundaries and should be performed and enjoyed by all who participate, either as a performer or as a listener. Emanating from African American spirituals and heavily influenced by the early New Orleans jazz musicians, Gospel music has been around for hundreds of years and has a sound, soul and joy all its own. Gospel songs add joy and happiness to our worship and other special events. It is universal in acceptance.

These easy duets are designed to allow the average to advanced players the opportunity to perform ten familiar Gospel songs in school, in church or any social occasion. No accompaniment is necessary. They may be played by any combination of woodwind, brass, string or mallet percussion instruments.

Below is an instrumentation guide that tells you the appropriate book to purchase for your instrument.

Most of all have fun and enjoy making music.

James Curnow
Composer/arranger

Instrumentation Guide

<u>C Instruments</u> (CMP 1224-07-400) Violin, Piccolo, Flute, Oboe, or any mallet percussion instrument.

<u>B♭ Instruments</u> (CMP 1226-07-400) Clarinet, Bass Clarinet, Cornet, Trumpet, Flugel Horn, Tenor Saxophone, Trombone T.C., Euphonium/Baritone T.C., Tuba T.C. (play second part only).

<u>E♭ Instruments</u> (CMP 1225-07-400) Alto Clarinet, Alto Saxophone, Baritone Saxophone (play second part only), Tenor (Alto) Horn, Tuba T.C. (play second part only).

<u>Horn F/E♭</u> (CMP 1227-07-400) F Horn, E♭ Horn, English Horn

<u>Bass Clef Instruments</u> (CMP 1228-07-400) Cello, Double Bass (play second part only), Bassoon, Trombone, Euphonium/Baritone, Tuba (play second part only).

SWING LOW, SWEET CHARIOT

Arr. by **James Curnow** (ASCAP)

AMAZING GRACE

Arr. by **James Curnow** (ASCAP)

EVERY TIME I FEEL THE SPIRIT

Arr. by **James Curnow** (ASCAP)

HE'S GOT THE WHOLE WORLD IN HIS HANDS

Arr. by **James Curnow** (ASCAP)

FACE TO FACE

Arr. by **James Curnow** (ASCAP)

GO, TELL IT ON THE MOUNTAIN

Arr. by **James Curnow** (ASCAP)

I'M SO GLAD, JESUS LIFTED ME

Arr. by **James Curnow** (ASCAP)

NOBODY KNOWS THE TROUBLE I'VE SEEN

Arr. by **James Curnow** (ASCAP)

STEAL AWAY

Arr. by **James Curnow** (ASCAP)

SWEET BY AND BY

Arr. by **James Curnow** (ASCAP)